T0023872

365 DAYS OF

inspiration

DAILY GUIDANCE FOR
A MORE MOTIVATED YOU

Robyn Martin

365 DAYS OF INSPIRATION

Copyright © Summersdale Publishers Ltd, 2022

Text by Olivia Coppin

Shooting stars © Victoria_vector_art/Shutterstock.com

An Hachette UK Company
www.hachette.co.uk

Vie Books, an imprint of Summersdale Publishers Ltd
Part of Octopus Publishing Group Limited
Carmelite House
50 Victoria Embankment
LONDON
EC4Y 0DZ
UK

www.summersdale.com

Printed and bound in China

ISBN: 978-1-80007-444-6

Substantial discounts on bulk quantities of Summersdale books are available to corporations, professional associations and other organizations. For details contact general enquiries: telephone: +44 (0) 1243 771107 or email: enquiries@summersdale.com.

To ....

From ....

introduction

Welcome to this book, and congratulations, for you have already taken the first steps toward unlocking inspiration by having a sense of openness and curiosity. You currently stand on the start line of a journey into the unknown. You have no idea what you will find within yourself and how your mind may flourish. How exciting!

Seeking inspiration is not only for those on creative endeavours. Feeling inspired also helps us to embrace new opportunities, to transcend self-imposed limitations on our capabilities and to take action to achieve goals. It can be found in anything and anyone when we start to look for it. With an inspired outlook, everyday interactions and experiences can become a source of joy and learning.

Nestled within these pages are tips for every day of the year, to help inspire you to live as your most enthusiastic, motivated, creative self. You may choose to read them in order, following the seasonal changes and flow of the year, or you may prefer to dip in and out, allowing yourself to trust you will find whatever inspiration you need that day. Whichever way you choose to read these tips, know that all it takes is commitment to one small act to transform your day, and your mindset, into something magical.

january

Today is your day!
Your mountain is waiting,
so get on your way.

DR SEUSS

Set aside a jar or prepare a journal to be filled with a new note anytime you encounter something that inspires you. Contribute to it every day, and you'll find that you have a treasure chest of inspiration to return to, any time you need it.

Take a quiet moment, close your eyes and visualize yourself achieving something. It could be as simple as lacing your trainers up as you prepare to go for a jog, or as grand as succeeding in your biggest life goals. Bask in the sensation, imagining all the details and how you feel in that moment.

Look up as you walk around today: at the sky, the architecture, the trees, the homes you pass that are each filled with unique lives. Allow yourself to adopt a new perspective by becoming more aware of your surroundings.

Listen to a new genre of music. Put on a pre-made playlist that may introduce you to new artists and songs, or switch up your regular radio station for something different.

Tell a loved one about the ways in which they inspire you, and all the reasons you love them. Notice how spreading gratitude leaves you feeling uplifted and energized.

••• 07 •••

Have a notepad by your bed to quickly note down any dreams as soon as you wake. In the light of day, you may find new meaning and inspiration within them.

Phone a relative or friend and ask them questions beyond the everyday. Perhaps you could ask about their childhood, obstacles they have overcome, their aspirations or what inspires them. As well as being inspirational, it may deepen your connection and empathy.

Pay close attention to the opportunities that arise today. Do you find yourself automatically turning down invitations or not offering your time to others? Be open to the possibility of new experiences – who knows how they may inspire you?

Take a different route to work or to the shops. It may not be the most direct route, but shaking up your routine will feel refreshing and may lead to new discoveries.

Choose a topic that intrigues you or an area you lack knowledge in, such as a specific historical event or philosophical principle, and read up on it.

The good news is that you don't know how great you can be! How much you can love! What you can accomplish! And what your potential is!

ANNE FRANK

Pay attention to nature today. Observe how you interact with the natural world around you, and vice versa. What creatures and plants are you co-existing with, and what can you learn from them?

When you are in your rocking chair talking to your grandchildren many years from now, be sure you have a good story to tell.

AMAL CLOONEY

Enquire about local volunteering opportunities. Is there a way you could engage more with your community and give back to those around you? If you can't commit to regular hours, most charities and organizations are grateful for an extra pair of hands in busy periods.

Think of a time when you achieved something you are proud of. Be your own inspiration.

Shake up your body and mind with a new type of sport or exercise class. For example, you could try salsa dancing, ultimate Frisbee or Tai-Chi. Search for group sessions in your local area to meet others or try a YouTube tutorial at home.

Try a free-writing exercise. Set a timer for 5 or 10 minutes and simply begin writing whatever appears in your mind. It doesn't have to be grammatical or structured, or to even make sense. The only rule is – don't stop writing!

I'm not going to continue knocking that old door that doesn't open for me. I'm going to create my own door and walk through that.

AVA DUVERNAY

Make a conscious choice not to fill the small gaps in your day with a screen. Whenever you are waiting or have time to kill, see what you can find from the world around you to entertain you instead.

••• (21) •••

Cook a new recipe. Whether you're an experienced chef or not, pick a delicious-looking recipe that feels outside of your comfort zone and go for it!

••• (22) •••

Go for a walk. Whatever the weather, however busy your day is, commit to spending some time – even just 5 minutes – just stretching your legs and being mindful of your surroundings.

••• (23) •••

Be bold and playful with your outfit today. Don't be afraid of others' judgements. Allow your fashion choices to represent exactly who you want to be.

The best way to get started is to quit talking and begin doing.

WALT DISNEY

Take a train ride or bus journey, and watch the world pass by. Allow yourself to get lost in the landscape, and be inspired by the idea of all the lives you are just passing through.

••• (30) •••

Think about any public figures who inspire you, and see if they have a biography or autobiography that you can read.

••• (31) •••

Ask yourself: "If I were to stop growing as a person, would I be happy with who I am?" Use any thoughts that arise as your inspiration to keep learning and evolving.

february

Try a food that you've never had before. Browse the "World Foods" aisle in the supermarket for new cuisines and snacks.

Vocalize, internalize or write down some affirmations, such as "I am loved", "I am grateful", "I am brave". You don't need to choose statements that resonate with you already – instead you might like to pick sentiments that you aspire to feel and believe. Watch how, if you're open, they will settle in your mind and body.

Arrange a visit to a museum. When there, take your time and commit to absorbing all the information that they have on offer. After your visit, recount at least five things that you learned.

Get up to watch the sunrise. Enjoy the still of the earth, the quiet of the land and the magnitude of the sun's unwavering strength. This immense natural act that occurs every day may inspire you to notice the endless possibilities for new beginnings and the transience of harder times.

Learn that new skill. Whatever it is that you've always had your eye on – a language, an instrument, a dance – today is the day to make the first move. Enquire about lessons or look up video tutorials to get you started.

Treat yourself to your favourite snack. Close your eyes and focus on the taste. Simply enjoy! Allow this slice of delight to put you in a positive mindset and act as a reminder to appreciate the little things.

••• (07) •••

Have a conversation with someone from a different generation. Whether older or younger, they may open your eyes to new perspectives.

••• (08) •••

Rediscover a much-loved storybook from your childhood and remember the time when your imagination had no limits.

••• (09) •••

Buy yourself a bunch of flowers. Watch them bloom and bring life into your home or office. The smell, shapes and colours will inspire you to find beauty in your day.

It isn't where you came from. It's where you're going that counts.

ELLA FITZGERALD

Do some exercise! Moving your body, however gently, increases blood flow to your brain and helps stimulate productivity, and the endorphins will boost your mood.

Book a trip somewhere new, whether that's abroad, to a country with an entirely different culture to your own, or just the next town over that you've never visited properly before. Who knows how you will be inspired and what you will discover when you broaden your horizons?

Try your hand at poetry. Write a few lines about how you're feeling or an encounter in your day. It doesn't have to rhyme or a fit a specific structure, just allow the words and emotions to flow. You may be surprised how poetic you can be when you give yourself the opportunity.

Witness all the examples of love around you. Between friends, lovers, pets and owners, parents and children. Appreciate what a powerful emotion it is and how it has inspired so much art and many acts of kindness around the world. How can love inspire you today?

At the end of the day, try to recap on something you learned today. It might be a news story or a fact about a friend. Be reminded that each and every day you are growing and learning.

Choose an item on your to-do list and do it. No matter how small, get it done, tick it off and get the ball of productivity rolling.

Look at the world through the lens of an artist today. Watch how the light falls and the multitude of colours that fill even the most mundane landscapes. If you were going to capture your surroundings in an artwork, how might that inspire you to view them differently?

Do a crossword puzzle. It will help fire up your brain, expand your vocabulary and test your general knowledge.

••• (19) •••

Watch a foreign-language film or TV show. It's a great way to dip into new cultures, absorb other languages and expand your knowledge of the world. Choose a subtitled version over dubbing to get a better grasp of the original language, and to ensure full concentration.

••• (20) •••

Drink enough water today. The recommended daily allowance for adults is 2 litres, or 8 glasses. Staying hydrated is important for many reasons, including maximizing brain function, so start building this habit today.

Nothing is impossible.
The word itself says
"I'm possible!"

AUDREY HEPBURN

Write a letter to your younger self. Consider including the lessons you have learned throughout the years, what memories you cherish most and what advice you would give to them.

Clear out your email inbox. Get rid of junk mail and leave as few as you can unread. Even creating this virtual space can help take a weight off and make you feel lighter.

If you were a character in a story, what would your main traits be? List the key components of your personality, and what makes you you. Think about your overarching goals in the story and what flaws might hold you back.

Change your socks or underwear halfway through the day. Feel how it gives you a new lease of life for the afternoon!

Try out a new perfume or scent.

••• 27 •••

Attend an inspirational talk, in real life or online. Allow the professionals to motivate you and inspire you with their tales. Who knows what spark they may unlock within you? All you have to do is show up.

Try a meat- and dairy-free day. Explore new flavours and ways your diet could be made more environmentally-friendly. You may be inspired to keep the new dishes in your life, and to make a plant-based day a weekly occurrence.

Watch a film with no distractions. Get fully immersed in the world of the film, and be inspired by the creativity of the craftspeople behind it.

••• (05) •••

Clear out any clothes that don't make you feel ten out of ten, and donate them to charity, or friends and family.

••• (06) •••

Learn a few simple phrases in a new language. Expand your mind and communication skills.

••• (07) •••

Create a savings pot, whether it is a jar for pennies or a savings bank account, and set a goal amount to save. You might want to decide what you will spend it on, in order to stay inspired to keep saving.

Spend 8 minutes gently stretching. In just a short time you will recognize where you're holding tension and how your body truly feels. Bringing your mind back into your body can help you feel more grounded and more attentive to the present moment.

Be the change you want to see happen.

ARLEEN LORRANCE

••• (10) •••

If you normally work sitting down, try a standing desk. How will a new perspective inspire you today?

••• •••

Visit a public garden. Meander through the displays and revel in the artistry of nature's colours and shapes. The arrangements might inspire you on how you can add colour and greenery to your home space.

Let us make our future now, and let us make our dreams tomorrow's reality.

MALALA YOUSAFZAI

••• (13) •••

Browse in stores you don't usually shop in. Even if they're outside of your budget, you can be inspired by designs, patterns and styles.

••• (14) •••

Write a list of books you would like to read. Contribute to it every time you hear a recommendation and you'll have a plethora of ideas if you are ever seeking inspiration.

••• (15) •••

Make a promise to yourself today to be open-minded. Allow other possibilities to flourish and to hear out the opinions of others.

••• (16) •••

Join a forum for a topic you're interested in or that discusses a challenge you find yourself facing. Find comfort and inspiration in those who have similar interests and experiences to you.

••• (17) •••

Create a logo for yourself. If you were a brand or had a product, what would it look like? What images and styles would best capture your essence?

Go to a playground and play! Go on the swings and monkey bars and roundabout. Embrace playfulness and observe how it alters your mood and outlook.

Do not allow people to dim your shine because they are blinded. Tell them to put sunglasses on.

LADY GAGA

··· ···

If you find yourself stuck for inspiration today, do something completely different to the task at hand, such as take a shower or tidy up. Complete an alternative, mindless activity to shake off the feeling of being unproductive.

··· ···

Flick through a stack of magazines, cutting out anything that sparks a reaction in you. You could scrapbook these images or pin them to a board, so they're on hand whenever you need a nugget of inspiration.

Write a letter to your future self. What are your hopes for that version of you? What do you want them to remember about where you are now? Use the thought of your future self as your drive to be the best you can be today.

Go to a car boot sale or flea market. Be inspired to upcycle and create something new from pre-loved items.

•••(24)•••

Read some literature out loud. Is it freeing to hear it aloud? Does it take on more meaning?

*If my mind can conceive it,
and my heart can believe
it – then I can achieve it.*

MUHAMMAD ALI

Send a care package to a loved one. Take time to be as thoughtful as possible about what they would appreciate. How might this action inspire you to take care of those around you more often?

Use your fanciest cutlery and crockery, just for you. Watch it elevate an everyday experience and turn the mundane into something special.

••• (28) •••

Try a new nickname for yourself. Perhaps a new alias will inspire a new attitude.

••• (29) •••

Get messy. Splash in a puddle, try finger painting or roll in the mud. Experience the enjoyment of complete freedom!

Even the worst days have an ending, and the best days have a beginning.

JENNIFER COLETTA

Read some poetry. There is a poem to cover every mood and taste. Experiment with a few styles and writers until you come across one that resonates and inspires you.

april

Buy some crafting materials, such as colourful pens and card paper. Have the materials ready, because you never know when the inspiration to create will appear!

Get up an hour earlier than usual. Create more time for yourself to squeeze every last drop of life out of the day ahead.

03

You are never too old to set another goal or to dream a new dream.

LES BROWN

04

Have a massage, or try self-massage. Massages allow your nervous system to slow down, and when you're more relaxed there's more space to feel positive and inspired.

• • ● **05** ● • •

Write down five key things that happened in your day yesterday. What about the day before? Last Monday? How much are you paying attention to your own life? What events stay with you and appear most important in your days?

Think up an invention. What tool or app would you find useful in your day-to-day?

Switch up your regular breakfast, or add it to your day if you usually skip it. You could even have something not typically deemed "breakfast food". See how it sets your day up differently.

Research the people who inspire the people who inspire you. Think about celebrities who you look up to, and most of them will have been asked in an interview about their own inspirations.

Try to be a rainbow
in someone else's cloud.

MAYA ANGELOU

Book a retreat. It could be purely for relaxation, to create mental space or centred around a hobby. Take a few days to give your body and mind a chance to reset, or get stuck into your passion.

Spend time on the presentation of your food today. How can this essential life force be made into art?

••• (17) •••

Allow yourself to be bored. See what arises when you're not constantly occupying yourself.

••• (18) •••

Listen to songs that you haven't heard before, choosing them only by song titles that appeal to you. You might be introduced to new artists and sounds.

●●● (19) ●●●

Take yourself on a date. Make an effort just for yourself and indulge in whatever you would like to do.

If you're a list-maker, try a new format. For example, swap a checklist for a mind map, or change tick boxes to shaded circles when complete. Even a minor switch up in your go-to habits can give you a new perspective.

••• (21) •••

Play a children's game, such as Hide and Seek, Stuck in the Mud, or It! Unleash your inner child and see how it inspires you to reignite a playfulness in your adult life.

••• (22) •••

Pick an item in your immediate surroundings and write a short story or poem about it.

••• (23) •••

Adjust the lighting in your house or workspace. Try lamps as opposed to overhead lights, and introduce colourful or patterned shades for a new vibe. Watch how changing the lighting affects the mood and inspires a new atmosphere.

24

If you were a superhero, what power would you have and how would you help the world? Think about, in its essence, ways you could bring this into your day now?

25

Try an electricity-free hour — or longer! Reconnect with other ways of living and communicating.

If I cannot do great things, I can do small things in a great way.

MARTIN LUTHER KING JR

Read up on a religion you know little about. You may be inspired by the key pillars of their faith, and gain more understanding toward your worldly neighbours.

• • • (28) • • •

Learn a new word and try to use it in conversation today.

••• (29) •••

Build a den in your home or garden, out of
cushions and blankets. Enjoy the innocence of this
creation and the tranquillity of the safe space.

Make a conscious decision to let go of something
that no longer serves you. Perhaps it could be
an emotion, a habit or a relationship. Find the
strength to shake off that which is holding you
back from being your brightest, most inspired self.

may

Tick off some useful but often neglected tasks, such as bleeding the radiators, checking the car oil and cleaning inside the fridge. These mini accomplishments will inspire you to feel on top of your own life.

Buy a disposable camera and use it this week instead of a digital one. How might you capture moments differently when the process is more precious?

••• (03) •••

Meditate on your happiest memories for a while. Allow them to fill you up with joy and carry you through your day in a positive, grateful mindset.

 ••• (04) •••

Spend time naked today. Discover how comfortable you feel in your own skin. Can you feel liberated? Powerful? How are you inspired when you're connected to the basics of what it is to be a human being?

Experiment with a new style of handwriting. It may even affect the words you write, when your hand is more considered.

••• 06 •••

Try silence today. Notice how your thoughts alter when they're not vocalized. Can you reach a point where your mind feels calm and orderly?

••• 07 •••

Watch a film that is outside of the usual genres you watch.

Set a small budget and set out to buy something from a charity shop. Your money is going toward a good cause, and it might inspire you to make an unusual purchase.

Visit a historical building. Learn about the people who would have created it and all the lives that have passed through since. Be inspired by the history that allows you to be here today.

••• (10) •••

Someone is sitting in the shade today because someone planted a tree a long time ago.

WARREN BUFFETT

••• (11) •••

Think about the layout of your workspace. Is it conducive to inspiration? How could you adjust the colour themes and layout to make you more productive?

••• (12) •••

Use an object to keep your hands occupied, such as a stress ball, tension toy or fidget spinner. This will allow your mind to focus better and maintain productivity.

**You define your own life.
Don't let other people
write your script.**

OPRAH WINFREY

Listen to your instincts today. Trust your gut to
make decisions and see where they take you.

Try a new hands-on hobby, such as knitting, crochet, whittling or pottery. Be inspired by your ability to create something physical.

••• (21) •••

Unsubscribe to unwanted emails en masse – right now. The process is so quick and soon it will declutter your day-to-day.

Real change, enduring change, happens one step at a time.

RUTH BADER GINSBURG

Think of an item you love — a piece of furniture, an item of clothing, a snack food — and look into how it is made or grown. Be inspired by the processes behind what you treasure most.

••• 24 •••

Carve out some alone time today. When you have time to be undisturbed, you can listen to your own mind more clearly.

Take a cold-water plunge. The shock will reset your whole body, and leave you feeling bright and refreshed. Alternatively, turn your water temperature right down just before you get out of the shower, for the same inspiring blast.

**Wake up determined.
Go to bed satisfied.**

DWAYNE JOHNSON

··· (27) ···

Visit a local, independent store. It can be inspiring to witness entrepreneurs and business ventures in action and see how people have achieved their dreams. Plus, it's always uplifting to support local!

··· (28) ···

Get a manicure. You will feel more polished, which in turn may inspire a new attitude.

··· (29) ···

Eat at least five portions of fruit and vegetables today. Making sure you're stocked up on vitamins and minerals is essential for brain function.

Don't try to lessen yourself for the world; let the world catch up to you.

BEYONCÉ

If you have a creative craft, allow yourself to create purely for the fun of it today. Don't think about the opinions of others or judge your own work. Reconnect with why you love it. Experimenting is liberating and can lead to inspiring discoveries.

june

This month brings another change of season and the opportunity to adapt anew to your shifting surroundings. How will you move with the changes?

Watch the clouds. Allow the sensation of them drifting along to represent your thoughts and feelings and serve as a reminder that everything passes.

If you sit for long periods at work, make sure to stand up and move around every 25 minutes. Not only is it better for your long-term health but it also keeps lethargy at bay and helps you to stay energized and productive.

Visit a library. Browse the hundreds of books on display without predetermined ideas of what you will read. Allow a cover or title to jump out at you. See where it takes you and what you can learn from it.

Some chapters are happy while others bring lessons to learn, but we always have the power to be the heroes of our own adventures.

JOELLE SPERANZA

Watch your very favourite film. Let it uplift you and make your heart feel joyous. Carry that into your day or evening with you.

Spend 5 minutes just focusing on your breathing. Be inspired by this miraculous system that keeps you alive every day.

Treat your day like a musical. Can you make up songs for what you're doing in that moment? Would the rhythm be upbeat or slower? Not only is it a fun exercise, but it's also a way to be more mindful about what activities and moods are pervading your day.

••• (09) •••

Create a mood board with interior designs or clothing styles that inspire you. It could be a physical pin board, or on a website such as Pinterest.

Write a list of mistakes you have made, however difficult to admit. Do not get bogged down by guilt or regret, but rather use them as a reminder to learn from your mistakes and grow as a person.

Research how other people are contributing to your field of work or creativity. Who is innovating? What boundaries are they pushing? How can they inspire you?

Take a photo of an everyday item and edit it to create something abstract. Be reminded how art is all around you and you are capable of creativity in all forms.

Plan a long weekend away with a friend. Make a list of fun activities and delicious places to eat, and take the time to bask in the specialness of close friendships.

Ask a child questions. Their out-of-the-box thinking can be very refreshing and shift your perspective completely.

Dreams don't have to just be dreams. You can make it a reality; if you just keep pushing and keep trying, then eventually you'll reach your goal.

NAOMI OSAKA

Nurture your body today. Pamper yourself with moisturizer, face masks or a bubble bath. If you feel treated well, your mind is free to unwind and explore.

••• (17) •••

Imagine that you are trying to inspire a friend who is stuck in a rut – what would you say to them?

••• (18) •••

Think of your goal for today. Write it on a post-it note and stick it somewhere – on your mirror, your fridge, the back of your mobile – to remind you throughout the day.

••• (19) •••

Grow something from seed. Be inspired watching it change and evolve every day.

Mix up your usual hot drink today. Swap tea for a herbal tea, a coffee for a mocha, or get one of the most ridiculous-sounding coffee-shop orders you can find. It might seem insignificant, but even a minor shake-up can breathe new life into your day.

Doodle. Spend a few minutes creating silly patterns and drawings for the joy of it. They might evolve into something unexpected.

••• (27) •••

Try a new piece of jewellery, or try wearing jewellery – or some other accessory – altogether if you don't usually. It might spark a new, jazzy attitude in you.

••• (28) •••

Choose a shape, for example a heart or a diamond, and watch out for all the times it appears in your day, including within nature. This will sharpen your focus on the world in front of you and make you more observant.

••• 29 •••

I believe that if you just stand up and go, life will open up for you. Something just motivates you to keep moving.

TINA TURNER

Smile, even if you don't feel like it. It tricks your brain and puts you in a better mood!

july

Do a few star jumps as soon as you get out of bed this morning. Get the blood pumping and feel ready to tackle the day!

Eat your favourite food from childhood. See what memories the taste unlocks and how they can inspire you afresh today.

··●(03)●··

Go on a date. It could be a first date, or with a long-term partner or with a friend. Whoever it is with, get excited, ask the bigger questions and revel in the enjoyment of someone else's company.

··●(04)●··

Belief creates the actual fact.

WILLIAM JAMES

··●(05)●··

Do some colouring in. This peaceful activity will allow your mind to wander and explore as you unwind.

Read a blog or article by someone in a field that interests you.

•••(07)•••

Adjust your workspace. Rearrange or organize your desk, add a plant, adjust your seat height. Little changes can make a big impact to your productivity.

•••(08)•••

Go clothes shopping and try on styles and colours that are unusual for you. You never know what might suit you, and how you might be inspired to freshen up your look.

··· ···

Bounce ideas off other people, whether it's for a project, or merely a discussion of ideas and opinions. Embrace the perspective of others and allow it to inspire your own.

··· (10) ···

Make a list of things you would like to do before the year is out.

··· (11) ···

Create an artwork from your recycling. This will encourage you to find inspiration even in the most unlikely places.

It is never too late to be what
you might have been.

GEORGE ELIOT

Write an apology to someone for something that
you still regret. Making amends will help you to
feel lighter and inspire you to live as your best self
moving forward.

Life is like riding a bicycle. To keep your balance, you must keep moving.

ALBERT EINSTEIN

Listen to the sounds around you today, without judgement. For example, don't block out the noises you usually write off as irritants. Simply listen to the full soundscape that underscores your day.

• • • (16) • • •

Do a steam bath over a bowl, or drop some essential oils into the base of a steamy shower. Feel your lungs expanding and your body relaxing. This moment of mindfulness and deep breathing will help you to focus more clearly.

Write a list of all the things that you own or experience now that you wished for once upon a time. Pause for a moment to take stock of your life and appreciate all that it is filled with and how far you have come. Use this for inspiration to believe you can achieve whatever you put your mind to.

Look up which vegetables and fruits are in season. This may inspire you for recipe ideas, as well as helping you to eat in a more eco-friendly way.

Learn some simple phrases in sign language. It is a very handy skill to have, in order to create a more inclusive world for everyone, and dipping your toe might inspire you to learn more.

You get what you give.

JENNIFER LOPEZ

••• 21 •••

Write a short story about absolutely anything. Just start writing and see where your mind takes you and what worlds you can create.

••• (22) •••

Create a new cocktail or mocktail. Mix together your favourite flavours and discover a new drink to enjoy whenever you need a pick-me-up.

••• (23) •••

Find a new scent for your home. Using diffusers to add a fresh fragrance to your space can transform it, and subsequently how you feel inside it.

••• (24) •••

Go out just for the sake of it. Take a walk where the only purpose is to wander and see what you find.

Get a good night's sleep. Avoid screens in the hour before bed, use ear plugs and an eye mask if needed and allow yourself the recommended 7-9 hours of sleep. This will better your energy and brain function for tomorrow.

Keep your face always turned toward the sunshine and the shadows will fall behind you.

ANONYMOUS

Try an elevator pitch. Whether pitching your own work or idea, or someone else's, how can you condense it to its key components?

••• 28 •••

Choose a loved one with an upcoming birthday and make them a card, instead of buying one. How might your knowledge of this person's character inspire the design you create and the words you write inside it?

Update your CV, even if you have no intention of changing jobs. Collate your achievements, training and experiences all in one place. Being proud of all you have done is a great source of inspiration.

You can be everything. You can be the infinite amount of things that people are.

KESHA

• • • (31) • • •

Remember that the day is unwritten and the possibilities are endless. Today could be the best day of your life – go out and embrace it!

Take a cookery class. Learn new dishes or a different cuisine that you can bring into your weekly routine to mix it up.

••• (07) •••

Watch a dance show, such as ballet or hip-hop. Be inspired by how people can use their bodies as an expressive art form.

••• (08) •••

Dress smartly today. Make an effort, look your best and feel it shift your attitude.

••• •••

If you don't like the road you're walking, start paving another one!

DOLLY PARTON

••• •••

Wrap up and sleep under the stars. Find peace and inspiration in the magic of the universe and this moment in time.

••• (11) •••

Set yourself some short-, medium- and long-term goals. Have an idea of where you're heading and what you need to do to get there.

Pay attention to how your body responds to certain foods. What makes you feel sluggish? What makes you feel energized? What leaves you satisfied? Use this knowledge to stay at your peak and keep on top of your day.

••• (13) •••

Read, watch or listen to the news. Both the good and the bad can be inspiring, and encourage you to be a positive force in the world.

••• (14) •••

Write an acrostic poem, where the first letter of the lines spell out: INSPIRE.

••• (15) •••

Spend time around animals today. Be inspired by their playfulness and the way they listen to their instincts. If you don't have, or know anyone with, pets, go to the park and watch the squirrels and birds in their natural habitat.

••• (16) •••

Spend a few minutes holding the "Winner's Pose". Hold your hands above your head like you've just won a race. By emulating the feeling of pride and success, it will filter into your mindset.

**We must be willing to
let go of the life we had
planned so as to have the
life that is waiting for us.**

JOSEPH CAMPBELL

Have breakfast in bed. This treat will set you up
for an indulgent, joyful day.

••• (19) •••

Leave a positive review for a service you've received or goods you have bought. Your comments might inspire others to follow suit.

••• (20) •••

Ask how you can help today? In every situation, how can you assist? How can you make other people's lives better and the world a more positive, inspiring place?

••• (21) •••

Take the time to watch a busker perform. Instead of walking past, pause to enjoy their performance. Not only will it potentially inspire and uplift you, but it will also mean a lot to them.

Pick a word that you always have trouble spelling. Write it over and over until you're sure to remember how it is spelt. This tiny lesson will inspire you to see how quickly and easily you can overcome small obstacles.

••• (23) •••

Ask a friend or loved one, or a colleague whose style you admire, to choose your outfit for the day.

••• (24) •••

My mission in life is not merely to survive, but to thrive.

MAYA ANGELOU

••• (25) •••

Do a deep clean. Get to all the forgotten corners and tasks: hoover inside the kitchen drawers, wash the sofa cushions, flip your mattress. Make everything feel sparkling new.

••• (26) •••

Take an afternoon nap. Just 20 minutes can transform your energy levels and power you through the rest of the day.

••• (27) •••

Read your horoscope. The words may inspire you to view your circumstances differently or to look out for certain opportunities.

Your time is limited, so don't waste it living someone else's life.

STEVE JOBS

••• (29) •••

Get a haircut. Even just a trim will make you feel fresh, or if you're feeling bolder, ask the hairdresser for their recommendations on what would suit you for a complete restyle.

Write a letter of appreciation to your local emergency services. Taking the time to put into words and acknowledge their heroic work may inspire you to see the greatness of your local community, and encourage you to give back.

Do not judge today. Watch how your outlook can blossom when you allow yourself and others to exist without being critiqued or put down.

september

Welcome the new change of season. Pause to consider what aspects of this next chapter you are most excited about.

Decorate your front door. Give it a fresh coat of paint or a floral wreath with in-season flowers. Make it something you're excited to come home to.

**Success is not final, failure
is not fatal; it is the courage
to continue that counts.**

WINSTON CHURCHILL

Go on a roller coaster. The flood of adrenaline will
reset your body and clear your mind.

•••(05)•••

Think about what social causes matter to you. How
can you get involved in helping? Can you attend
a march or organize a fundraiser? How can you
inspire others to address the cause too?

Tip as much as you can to servers you encounter today. Let them know that you appreciate their hard work and inspire them to keep going.

••• (07) •••

When you wake up, take a few moments for yourself. Don't check your phone or jump straight out of bed. This morning, lie in the peaceful stillness and ease into your day mindfully. Watch how this sets today up on a calmer path.

Introduce yourself to someone new. Every connection is an opportunity for new insights, stories, relationships and memories.

Don't be afraid to push the boundaries.

PAULA RADCLIFFE

Go along with a friend to their hobby or an event that they're interested in, even if it is not your thing. It might open your eyes or inspire you, and when supporting a friend, there is nothing to lose in the process!

••• (16) •••

Look in the mirror and promise yourself, "Today will be a good day." Then go out and make it happen.

••• (17) •••

Consider who of the people you surround yourself with uplift and inspire you, and who don't bring out the best in you. Think about whether it's time to reevaluate your friendships. Letting people go can be tough, but it can lead to a brighter, lighter life.

••• (18) •••

Be spontaneous today. Don't make plans – just go with the flow!

Whatever you're working on, start with a very rough first draft. It doesn't matter how far from perfect it is – once you've got a draft version to go off it will be far easier to take the next steps.

No matter what you're going through, there's a light at the end of the tunnel.

DEMI LOVATO

• • • (21) • • •

Organize your clothes by colour. It might mix up the way you see your wardrobe and inspire new outfit choices.

If you were to write an autobiography, what would the key stories and lessons be so far? What sections would bring you most joy to revisit and which would be harder to write? And what new chapters are yet to be written?

Do a word search puzzle. Get your brain fired up and see what jumps out at you.

● ● ● (24) ● ● ●

Do a favour for someone without expecting anything in return.

● ● ● (25) ● ● ●

Prep your clothes and everything you need for the day, the night before. It will help you feel more relaxed and prepared in the morning, and set you up to win the day.

● ● ● (26) ● ● ●

Write an A-Z list of positive, inspiring words. It could be a rough scribble, or you could take time to decorate the words colourfully and pin it up somewhere to inspire you daily.

I can't change the direction of the
wind, but I can adjust my sails
to always reach my destination.

JIMMY DEAN

Take the first step in adopting a new healthy habit,
such as bettering your sleeping pattern, drinking
more water or getting more exercise. Whatever it
is, you can do this!

Engage with physical touch with those you love today. Hug friends, hold hands with your children or show support with a pat on the back. Watch how it makes you feel more connected to those you care about.

Frame something you're proud of, such as a piece of work or a certificate. Hang it up, pride of place, and be inspired by yourself.

october

Look at your calendar for the next month. Make sure you have at least five events that you are excited for. Even if that means scheduling a non-negotiable, self-care night in.

Watch some live music. Absorb the atmosphere and the experience of collective enjoyment. Be reminded how special moments can feel even better when shared.

Research your family tree. Understanding your history might inspire who you are tomorrow.

Use the checkout at the shops with a cashier, instead of an automated one. Even this brief interaction is an opportunity to meet someone new and shape your day differently.

You must do the things you think you cannot do.

ELEANOR ROOSEVELT

Pick a basic physical task to improve upon this week. For instance, you could focus on press ups, balancing on one leg or holding a plank position. Spend a few minutes practising each day and notice how quickly you can improve.

If you wear makeup, visit a beauty counter and ask them to do it for you. They may teach you new tips and techniques and introduce you to products best suited to your complexion and style.

••• (08) •••

Fill a bare wall with artwork. It could be posters, photographs or pieces of your own work. Transform it into a space you get passing enjoyment from looking at.

••• (09) •••

Even if you're feeling uninspired today, power through. Do the things that you think you are unable to, and watch inspiration come to you.

••• (10) •••

Get engaged with local politics. Find out who is advocating for things that matter to you in your area, and how you can get involved.

Carry out a random act of kindness, such as letting someone go in front of you in a queue or leaving money in the parking machine. It will boost your mood and spread positivity.

Choose confidence today. Even if you don't truly feel it, you can pretend. If you believe in yourself and your abilities, others will too. What might a more confident you be inspired to achieve?

Go people watching, in a park or a cafe window. Be inspired by people's outfits, by the acts of friendship you see, by the way they carry themselves.

List five things that make you completely unique to everyone else on the planet. It could be the placement of your freckles or the tone of your laugh. There is only one you in the whole world. Embrace your individuality and what sets you apart from everyone else.

Today's accomplishments were
yesterday's impossibilities.

ROBERT H. SCHULLER

Start laughing. Even if there's nothing funny
happening, just start laughing and the silliness of
the task might make it evolve into a real laugh.
Everything feels brighter after a hearty laugh.

Try to avoid mirrors today. Focus on how you feel, not what you look like.

Read a magazine from a genre you would never normally engage with. You will learn something new, and may be inspired in ways that you didn't expect.

When you ask people how they are today, really listen. And equally, when asked yourself, give an honest, considered answer. It will invite further conversation and deeper connection.

We need to take risks. We need to go broke. We need to prove them wrong, simply by not giving up.

AWKWAFINA

When you are in a public place, internally list a positive remark about all the strangers around you. Perhaps they have kind eyes or nice trainers or are interacting lovingly with their friend. Reframe your thinking to look for the good in people.

When you get into bed at the end of the day, think what you would do differently if you had the chance to do the day over. Use this as fuel to get the best out of tomorrow.

••● 28 ●••

Book in those routine healthcare check-ups, such as the dentist and optician. Being proactive in staying on top of your health is essential to making the most out of every day.

••● 29 ●••

Organize an evening with friends or family where the purpose is to reminisce. Spend the get-together discussing fond memories and sharing loving stories. It will keep the light of your friendship burning strong.

If you find you have a lull in energy and productivity in the afternoon, take yourself for a brisk walk and drink a warm, lightly caffeinated drink, such as a green tea. This will boost your mood, without draining you or impacting your sleeping pattern.

Play dress up. Put on a ridiculous outfit and walk around the house, just as a child does with fancy dress. The sillier the better to shake up your day!

november

Open the windows, whatever the weather. Let the fresh air flow in.

A lot of people are afraid to say what they want. That's why they don't get what they want.

MADONNA

Do something that scares you today. Feel the adrenaline rush, and allow it to make you feel capable of conquering whatever is holding you back.

••• (04) •••

Send someone a note praising their hard work. Encouraging others around you will in turn boost your own performance and make you strive to be an inspiration to others.

Set aside some time to go through your bank account and implement a budget. Take a look at your incomings and outgoings, and where there is room to save or spend. Staying on top of finances is crucial to minimizing anxiety and ensuring you feel organized.

Be yourself; everyone else is already taken.

OSCAR WILDE

··· (07) ···

Discuss with a healthcare professional if they advise any supplements for you. It is important to get all the vitamins and minerals in your diet, in order to maximize your performance each day.

Organize a "staycation". Plan an itinerary of local activities and create a schedule as if you were on holiday as a tourist. Be inspired to make the most of what's on your doorstep.

••• (09) •••

Sleep the other way round in bed tonight, and see if you gives you a new perspective.

••• (10) •••

Commit to improving your flexibility. Gentle stretching every day will loosen up your muscles and make your body feel better equipped to handle whatever the day throws at you. Consistency is key.

If you're on social media, take a break. Can you cut it out for a day? A whole week? See how your mindset changes and how you're inspired when you spend longer focused on the real world in front of you.

Ask a friend or family member who you respect to describe you in five adjectives. Be open to their answers and see if it matches up with how you see yourself.

••• (13) •••

It's better to be absolutely ridiculous than absolutely boring.

MARILYN MONROE

••• (14) •••

Visit an art gallery. Move away from more intellectual responses and focus on how you respond emotionally to the work on display. Feel how it moves you and in what ways it inspires you.

••• (15) •••

Put your headphones on, play your favourite music and be the protagonist of your own story.

Feed the birds. It's a tranquil, mindful activity that is sure to help you relax and be present, making way for a more inspired outlook.

Reach out to an old friend who you haven't spoken to in a long time. Not only might the path that their life has taken inspire you, but also by reconnecting with your past self you may unearth all the ways in which you have grown.

Watch a comedy show, either in real life or on screen. Laughter is the best way to loosen up and be inspired by the humour in humanity.

I have not failed. I've just found 10,000 ways that won't work.

THOMAS EDISON

Do not dim your own light or undervalue your perspective today, or any day. Vow to make a conscious effort to be honest about how you truly feel and rest assured that you can have no regrets when you're being your authentic self.

Do a sudoku puzzle. Shifting into logical, mathematical thinking might unlock a way to tackle a riddle in your own life.

Dance like nobody's watching. Overcome any self-consciousness to let loose and move your body in a way that feels good to you. Get those endorphins flowing and inspiration is sure to follow.

Set aside time to meditate today. Close your eyes and focus on your breathing and the feel of your physical body. Stay here as long as you need, quietening the mind and finding stillness.

Get to know your neighbours, if you don't already. You don't know what amazing people might be living right next door and how they might inspire your life.

The bad news is time flies.
The good news is you're the pilot.

MICHAEL ALTSHULER

••● ●••

Try to work using the Pomodoro Technique. Set a timer and work in focused, 25-minute intervals, taking short breaks in between. This will keep your mind fresh and aid productivity.

••● ●••

Buy a house plant. Being responsible for a living thing and watching it thrive can sometimes be a small inspiration to keep going that day.

••● 28 ●••

Spend some time upside down today. Hang off the sofa, or learn how to do a headstand. The flow of blood to the brain and the new perspective may be enlightening!

••• (03) •••

Brush your teeth using your non-dominant hand. Notice how hard-wired your brain is and what it feels like to challenge it.

••• (04) •••

Send a letter to yourself. Make the contents something that will inspire you in a few days' time.

••• (05) •••

Run as fast as you can! It doesn't have to be for long, only long enough to feel your heart pumping and to enjoy that childlike freedom.

••• (06) •••

If you see litter, pick it up and bin it. This little act may help you think about what a positive impact you can have on the world around you.

Believe you can and
you're halfway there.

THEODORE ROOSEVELT

Think about the characters that inspired you as a child. Consider what qualities they possessed, what you learned from them and whether they are still inspirational to you today.

Try a yoga class, online or in-person. The ancient practice is rooted in mindfulness and is designed to be suitable for everyone. Find the right class and you'll leave the mat feeling uplifted, stretched and inspired.

Prep your meals for the week ahead. It will put you in an organized mindset and give you extra time each day to spend working, creating, playing, relaxing or producing instead.

Write an acceptance speech for an award that you would like to win. Who would you thank for inspiring you?

Go to the theatre. There is so much to be inspired by: the plot's morals or themes, the skill of live performers and the artistry and teamwork of creative minds coming together.

You have brains in your head. You have feet in your shoes. You can steer yourself any direction you choose!

DR SEUSS

Bookmark any online article, or save any real-life copy, that offers you a spark of inspiration to reread anytime you want to return to a positive, motivated mindset.

Make a promise to yourself today to be fearless. You will speak up, you will go after what you want, you will be bold.

If you have a creative craft that you're interested in – writing, art, music – research the history of how it came to be a part of human life. Who were the key contributors to your favourite genre? What were the turning points in its history?

••• (17) •••

Give yourself permission to do only what you enjoy today. Do not feel pressured to do anything that doesn't bring you positivity or leave you feeling inspired.

We don't "have" a great day, we "make" it a great day!

FROSTY WESTERING

Describe all the people you love in three words each. What key qualities do you appreciate in them the most?

••• 20 •••

Sing your heart out. In the shower, in the car or in public for everyone to hear. Feel the release of inhibitions and the freeing nature that can allow room for your truest self.

··•(21)•··

Ask "why" a lot today. Ask yourself and others and see what the answers unearth.

··•(22)•··

Make a gift for a loved one, instead of buying it from a store. What can you create that they will cherish?

··•(23)•··

Watch a funny video. A little laugh can loosen you up and allow your creativity and productivity to flow.

••• (24) •••

Make a list of all the things you love about yourself.

••• (25) •••

Learn a new board game or card game and share it with family or friends. Set yourself up to make new memories with loved ones.

••• (26) •••

Call someone who might be lonely. If you can't think of anyone in your own life, there are charities who help connect isolated elderly people. Who knows how your conversation will unfold and what stories you will learn?

Where there is love and
inspiration, I don't think
you can go wrong.

ELLA FITZGERALD

Look in the mirror, into your eyes. Stay longer than usual, making a connection with yourself. See only what is truly there, rather than judging perceived flaws. How differently can you start to see yourself?

••• (29) •••

Teach someone something today. A fact, a skill, a recipe. Be an inspiration for others.

••• (30) •••

Look back upon the year that has just passed, revisiting what your aspirations were and all that you have gained and learned along the way.

••• (31) •••

Write a bucket list of all the things that you'd like to do in your lifetime, from places to visit to big achievements to silly things. It can be as epic as you want to make it. Allow it to inspire you to get out there and tackle every day.

conclusion

As we conclude our year of daily tips and reminders, I hope that you feel better equipped with a toolkit to help unlock inspiration. You may like to recollect which days you found most useful and the wonderful events and emotions that evolved as a result, and how you can incorporate them into your life moving forward.

Remember that our relationship with inspiration is not linear, and some days it can feel harder to find. That which inspires you one day may differ the next, and altogether alter over time as you grow. But these pages will always be here to return to, whenever you need them.

I wish you all the best with your onward journey, and hope that you continue to pursue a life that is inspired, and inspirational.

also available

365 DAYS OF CALM

ISBN: 978-1-80007-443-9

Robyn Martin

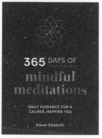

365 DAYS OF MINDFUL MEDITATIONS

ISBN: 978-1-80007-101-8

Karen Edwards

365 DAYS OF POSITIVITY

ISBN: 978-1-80007-102-5

Debbi Marco

365 DAYS OF KINDNESS

ISBN: 978-1-80007-100-1

Vicki Vrint

365 DAYS OF YOGA

ISBN: 978-1-78783-641-9

Have you enjoyed this book?
If so, find us on Facebook at
Summersdale Publishers, on Twitter
at @Summersdale and on Instagram
at @summersdalebooks and get in
touch. We'd love to hear from you!

www.summersdale.com